Date: 10/17/16

MEASURE IT!

Measuring Height

By T. H. Baer

Gareth Stevens
PUBLISHING

Please visit our website, www.garethstevens.com. For a free color catalog of all our high-quality books, call toll free 1-800-542-2595 or fax 1-877-542-2596.

Library of Congress Cataloging-in-Publication Data

Baer, T. H., author.
 Measuring height / T.H. Baer.
     pages cm. — (Measure it!)
 Includes index.
 ISBN 978-1-4824-3860-4 (pbk.)
 ISBN 978-1-4824-3861-1 (6 pack)
 ISBN 978-1-4824-3862-8 (library binding)
 1. Measurement—Juvenile literature. I. Title. II. Series: Measure it! (Gareth Stevens Publishing)
 QC90.6.B34 2016
 530.8—dc23
                                          2015027019

Published in 2016 by
Gareth Stevens Publishing
111 East 14th Street, Suite 349
New York, NY 10003

Copyright © 2016 Gareth Stevens Publishing

Designer: Laura Bowen
Editor: Ryan Nagelhout

Photo credits: Cover, p. 1 LWA/The Image Bank/Getty Images; pp. 2–24 (background texture) style_TTT/Shutterstock.com; p. 5 Christopher Hopefitch/Taxi/Getty Images; p. 7 Vstock LLC/Getty Images; p. 9 (football field) antpkr/Shutterstock.com; p. 9 (football) Pincarel/Shutterstock.com; p. 9 (1-foot ruler) Alhovik/Shutterstock.com; pp. 9, 11 (yardstick) John T Takai/Shutterstock.com; p. 11 (tape measure) Sashkin/Shutterstock.com; pp. 11, 13 (shrub) sirapob/Shutterstock.com; pp. 11, 13 (background) rangizzz/Shutterstock.com; pp. 13, 19 (tape measure) Andrey_Kuzmin/Shutterstock.com; p. 15 Jupiterimages/Stockbyte/Thinkstock.com; p. 17 Vladyslav Danilin/Shutterstock.com; p. 19 (coffee table) Fotosearch/Shutterstock.com; p. 21 Susan Law Cain/Shutterstock.com.

Printed in the United States of America

CPSIA compliance information: Batch #CW16GS: For further information contact Gareth Stevens, New York, New York at 1-800-542-2595.

Contents

Boldface words appear in the glossary.

How Tall?

How tall are you? Or how tall is the tree outside? We have to measure to find out! Height is a measurement of vertical distance. The tree is probably much taller than you are, but we often use the same **units** to measure both!

The Right Foot

We use many units to measure height. An inch (in) is the smallest measurement in US customary, or standard, units. Twelve inches is also equal to 1 foot (ft). One tool we use to measure is called a ruler. Most rulers are 1 foot long.

= 1 inch

Another tool used to measure height is called a yardstick. A yard (yd) is 3 feet long. That's how long a yardstick is! A yardstick is equal to three 1-foot rulers end to end. Three feet equal 36 inches.

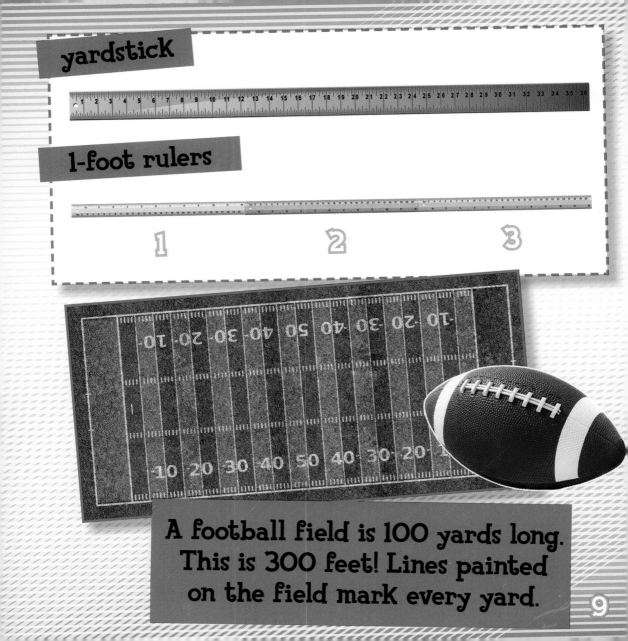

yardstick

1-foot rulers

1 2 3

A football field is 100 yards long. This is 300 feet! Lines painted on the field mark every yard.

Measure That Shrub!

Let's measure this **shrub**.
It's a bit taller than a yardstick.
We need a tool to measure
more than 3 feet. A tape
measure is a tool that **stretches**
out to measure things. It's
much longer than a yardstick.

?

3 feet
or 1 yard

tape measure

Feet and inches are used together to measure height. Let's put the tape measure up to the shrub. How tall is it? The tape measure says it's 3 feet and 3 inches tall. How many inches is the shrub?

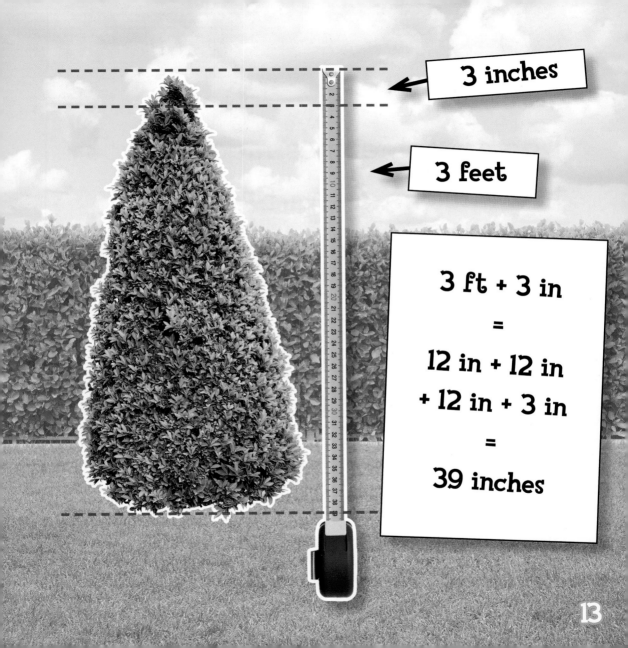

3 inches

3 feet

3 ft + 3 in

=

12 in + 12 in
+ 12 in + 3 in

=

39 inches

13

Doctors sometimes measure your height using a chart. It might hang on the wall, and you stand in front of it. The chart tells how tall you are! This height chart says the boy is 48 inches tall. That means he's 4 feet tall!

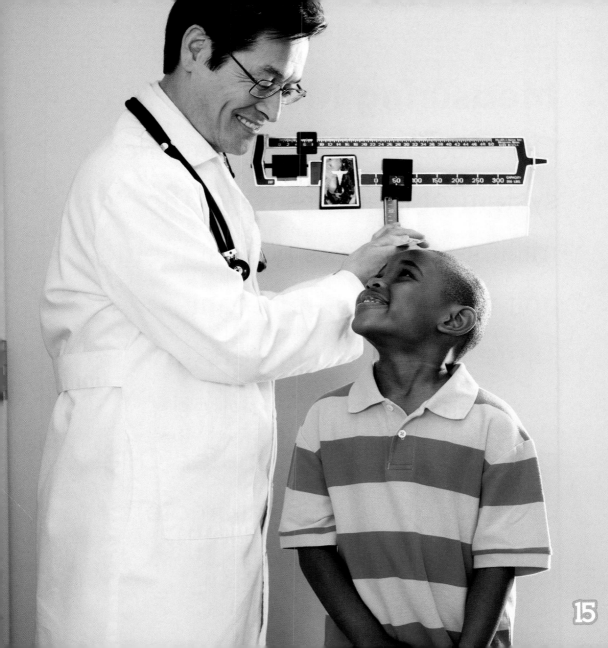

Measuring Metric

Other countries use the metric system of measurement. The millimeter is the smallest metric unit that measures height. There are 10 millimeters in a centimeter. A hundred centimeters make 1 meter. One meter is also 1,000 millimeters.

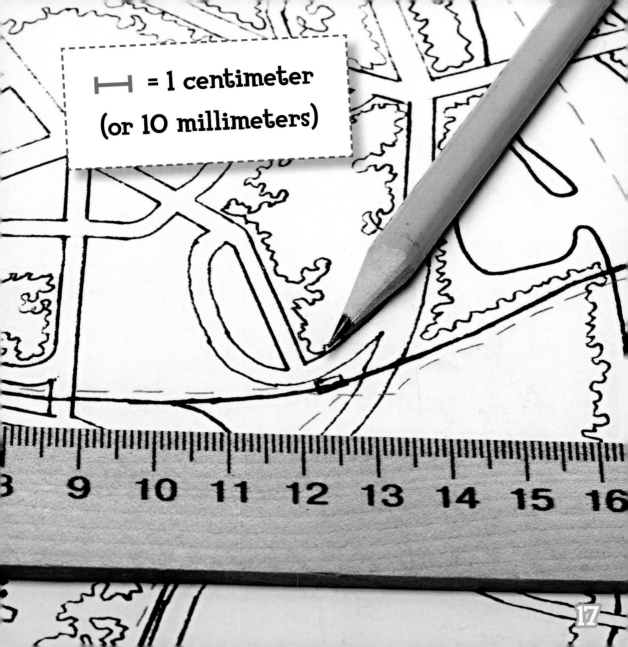

⊢ = 1 centimeter
(or 10 millimeters)

Let's use metric and US customary units to measure the height of this table. The tape measure shows us that the table is 24 inches tall. We can **convert** that to metric units. The table is about 61 centimeters tall!

conversion

1 inch = 2.54 centimeters

23 24

24 inches = about 61 centimeters

What's the Story?

People sometimes use a unit called a story to measure tall buildings. A story is one floor of a building. It's not an exact measurement, though. Buildings often have different story heights! It takes a lot more measuring to figure out how tall a 10-story building is!

3rd story

2nd story

1st story

21

Glossary

convert: to change from one unit to another

shrub: a woody plant smaller than a tree

stretch: to reach or pull out

unit: a uniform amount for measuring

For More Information

Books

Gardner, Robert. *How High Is High? Science Projects with Height and Depth.* Berkeley Heights, NJ: Enslow Elementary, 2015.

Parker, Victoria. *How Tall Is Tall? Comparing Structures.* Chicago, IL: Heinemann Library, 2011.

Websites

Kids Math
ducksters.com/kidsmath/units_of_measurement_glossary.php
Find out more about different units of measurement on this site.

Measurement Worksheets
e-learningforkids.org/math/lesson/measuring-distances/
Test your measuring skills with worksheets on this site.

Unit Lengths
numbernut.com/prealgebra/units-length.php
Find more conversions for different measurements here.

Index